# Skunk at Hemlock Circle

SMITHSONIAN'S BACKYARD

*For my niece and nephew,*
*Hana and Cooper Jones, with love.*
        —V.S.

*I dedicate this book to the*
*little furry animals inside all of us.*
        —A.D.

Book Design: Shields & Partners, Westport, CT

First Edition
10 9 8 7 6 5 4 3 2 1
Printed in Singapore

*Acknowledgements:*
   Our very special thanks to Dr. Charles Handley of the department of vertebrate zoology at the
Smithsonian's National Museum of Natural History for his curatorial review

*Library of Congress Cataloging-in-Publication Data*

Sherrow, Victoria.

Skunk at Hemlock Circle / by Victoria Sherrow ;
illustrated by Allen Davis.
         p.          cm.
Summary: Skunk comes out at night to search the backyard for his dinner.
         ISBN 1-56899-031-6
1. Skunks — Juvenile fiction.  [1. Skunks — Fiction.]
I. Davis, Allen, ill.  II. Title.
         PZ10.3.S387Sk 1994
         [E] — dc20

93-35511
CIP
AC

# Skunk at Hemlock Circle

*by Victoria Sherrow*

*Illustrated by Allen Davis*

**Sound**prints

*A Division of Trudy Management Corporation, Norwalk, Connecticut*

It is a hot August evening. Skunk wakes up and crawls out of his underground burrow. He takes a drink from the small stream flowing through a grove of hemlock trees. Night is his time to explore the backyard of the white house on Hemlock Circle. There, he has always been able to find plenty of insects and plants to eat for dinner.

His bushy tail sways as he boldly struts out of the woods and into the grassy backyard. Under the shimmering crescent moon, the white stripes on Skunk's back stand out against his inky-black fur.

Because Skunk depends more on his hearing than his eyesight in the dark, he listens for sounds of his evening meal. He hears the hooting of an owl, and the echo of a singing whippoorwill.

9

*"Chirp, chirp, chirp!"* The loud chirping of a lone cricket rings out among the evening noises. Sure enough, it hops and lands just under Skunk's eyes. Skunk springs toward it, landing on his front feet. He just misses as the cricket leaps out of his reach.

Skunk is about to pounce again. The sound of movement on the lawn interrupts his hunt.

A raccoon is prowling through the backyard. Skunk stands completely still, waiting. The raccoon comes closer, but Skunk does not run to hide. He arches his back and raises his bushy tail. At the same time, he stamps his front feet, clicks his teeth, and cries, *"Churr-churr-churr!"*

13

14

Suddenly, the raccoon recognizes Skunk's warning. He rushes out of the yard. The raccoon has tangled with skunks before. Skunk lowers his tail and listens again for nearby crickets. Instead, a hushed stillness settles on the yard.

Still hungry, Skunk heads for more hemlock trees on the other side of the yard. There, he has often found plump caterpillars to eat.

As Skunk searches around the trunk of a tree, he hears the rustling of dried pine needles. Something else is coming! An opossum approaches the hemlock, also looking for food.

19

Skunk freezes, and raises his tail high. He clicks his teeth together again in warning.

The opossum creeps closer. Seeing Skunk, his mouth opens, showing his sharp, pointy teeth. *"HISS! HISS!"*

Skunk's tail grows stiff to its very tip. Quickly, he twists his bottom around and fires a wet, yellowish spray through the air. It showers the opossum in the face.

The opossum is blinded by Skunk's spray. He rolls around on the ground trying to rub the smelly wetness off his fur. The smell does not go away, however. Giving up, the opossum races out of the yard.

Skunk lowers his tail. Now hungrier than ever, he goes back
to hunting for food. Just then, a mouse scurries across the grass.

Silently Skunk follows the mouse in between rows of large green plants. He pokes his head this way and that, but the mouse is nowhere to be found.

Looking up, he spots something familiar — giant stalks of corn tower over him. He is in the backyard's vegetable garden. The tall stems grow toward the sky. On them are ripe, juicy ears. At last, Skunk has found his dinner — dinner which will not escape him.

Skunk tugs at an ear of corn at the lowest end of the stalk. He shreds the husks and munches on the plump, yellow kernels. Unseen, the forgotten mouse darts out of the garden. But Skunk is content. Many ears are within his reach.

Stars glitter across the sky. Soon Skunk's busy night will come to an end. A long day's sleep awaits him.

## About the Skunk

The skunk depicted in this story is the striped skunk, commonly found in most of the United States and southern Canada. Living in rural and suburban areas, these noctural animals make their homes under buildings as well as in burrows abandoned by other animals, such as woodchucks, badgers, and foxes. Full-grown striped skunks are about the size of an average cat. Striped skunks are best known for their smelly spray that comes from two sacs (bag-like containers) under their tails. The bold white stripes on their backs and heads make them easy for other animals to spot, so enemies know to keep away.

## Glossary

*burrow:* a hole in the ground that an animal digs to use as a home.

*crickets:* leaping insects. Only the males make a shrill, chirping noise.

*grove:* a small group of trees often without underbrush.

*husk:* the covering, sometimes layered, of some fruits, nuts, seeds, and vegetables, such as ears of corn.

*insect:* a small animal, often with wings, that has three pairs of legs and three body sections.

*kernel:* a grain or seed of a grain plant.

*stream:* a small body of running water.

## Points of Interest in this Book

*pp. 4-5* wild mint.
*pp. 6-7* clover.
*pp. 8-9* great horned owl.
*pp. 10-11* American Caesar's mushroom.

*pp. 10-11, 12-13, 16-17* dandelions.
*pp. 18-19* lichen, versicolor shelf fungus, shortleaf pine.
*pp. 22-33* sphinx moth, jack-o-lantern mushroom, buttercup.
*pp. 26-27* snail.

j P                                    4-95
Sherrow, Victoria

Skunk at Hemlock Circle

WITHDRAWN